Bands on the Sand

By Clem King

Beth and Rand
had a rock band.

Mandy and Fred
were in the band, too.

"Look, Rand!" said Beth.
"It's a band clash
on the sand!"

"We can win that!"
said Rand.

It was the day of
Bands on the Sand.

Beth and the band came down to the big band stand.

Beth and Rand sat
on the sand to see a band.

Mandy and Fred sat, too.

Then, Beth's band went
on the stand.

But a big wind came up!

"The big wind will not stop us!" said Rand.

Beth's band rocked
and rolled.

And they got the grand cup!

CHECKING FOR MEANING

1. Where was the band clash to be held? *(Literal)*

2. What did the band win? *(Literal)*

3. How do you think Beth and her band felt after Bands on the Sand? *(Inferential)*

EXTENDING VOCABULARY

sand	Where do we mostly see *sand*? How does it feel to walk on sand?
stand	What is the meaning of the word *stand* in this story? Can you use *stand* in another sentence to show a different meaning?
grand	Look at the word *grand*. How many sounds can you hear in this word? What is the meaning of the word *grand*? Can you think of other words that have a similar meaning? E.g special, fancy.

MOVING BEYOND THE TEXT

1. Do you think the sand was a good place to play in a band? Where do you think would be the best place to play? Why?

2. What instruments are usually played in a band? How many people can play in a band?

3. If you were in a band, which instrument would you like to play and why?

4. Would you rather play in a band or as a solo performer? Why?

SPEED SOUNDS

| ft | mp | nd | nk | st |

PRACTICE WORDS

Rand

band

and

sand

stand

Mandy

Bands

grand

wind